From Fear to Flourish:
AI and the Future of Creativity

UNLOCKING THE POTENTIAL OF AI IN CREATIVE WORK

Nurlan Mahmudov

ISBN: 9798328564281
First Edition: 2024

Disclaimer: The information in this book is provided for informational purposes only. The author and publisher make no representations or warranties with respect to the accuracy or completeness of the contents of this book and specifically disclaim any implied warranties of merchantability or fitness for a particular purpose. The advice and strategies contained herein may not be suitable for your situation. You should consult with a professional where appropriate. The author and publisher are not liable for any loss of profit or other commercial damages, including but not limited to special, incidental, consequential, or other damages.

Contents

<u>Introduction</u>

The AI Revolution

The world is amid a technological renaissance driven by rapid artificial intelligence (AI) advancements. From healthcare to finance, AI transforms industries by automating tasks, analyzing data, and providing once unimaginable insights. However, amidst these changes, one sector remains cautiously optimistic: the creative industry. Artists, writers, musicians, and designers are grappling with the implications of AI on their craft. Will AI replace human creativity, or will it be a powerful tool to enhance and expand our creative capabilities?

Defining Creativity in the AI Era

Creativity has always been considered a uniquely human trait, characterized by the ability to think outside the box, generate novel ideas, and express emotions that resonate with others. In the AI era, however, the definition of creativity is evolving. AI can now generate art, compose music, write poetry, and develop new recipes. But can these creations be considered genuinely creative? This book explores how AI is reshaping our understanding of creativity and how humans can harness this technology to push the boundaries of their creative endeavors.

The Fear Factor

The rise of AI has not been without its detractors. Many fear that AI will render human creativity obsolete, leading to a future where machines dominate the arts. These fears are rooted in several common misconceptions about AI and its capabilities. This chapter will delve into these concerns, examining why people fear AI and the misconceptions that fuel these fears. By addressing these issues head-on, we can begin to shift the narrative from one of fear to one of opportunity.

The Purpose of This Book

"From Fear to Flourish: AI and the Future of Creativity" is not just a book about technology; it's a manifesto for a new era of creativity. This book is for artists, writers, musicians, designers, and anyone who has ever felt uncertain about their place in a world increasingly influenced by AI. It is a call to action to embrace AI as a collaborator rather than a competitor and see it as a tool that can amplify human creativity rather than diminish it.

What You Will Learn

In the following chapters, we will explore the myths and realities of AI in the creative industry. We will examine how AI can enhance rather than replace creative jobs, produce meaningful and soulful work, and democratize creativity without diluting its quality. Through case studies, practical advice, and personal testimonials, this book will provide you with the knowledge and tools to integrate AI into your creative process.

You will learn about the various AI tools available for creative fields, from writing and visual arts to music and video production. We will address the cultural and psychological barriers to adopting AI and offer strategies for overcoming these challenges. You will also get a glimpse into AI's future trends and ethical considerations in creativity, preparing you to stay ahead in a rapidly evolving landscape.

A Journey from Fear to Flourish

This book is structured to take you on a journey. We will start by confronting the fears and misconceptions surrounding AI, then move on to explore the practical applications and benefits of AI in the creative process. By the end of this journey, you will be equipped with a new perspective on AI—a perspective that sees AI as an enabler of creativity, a tool that can help you flourish in your creative endeavors.

Join the Conversation

As you read this book, think critically about the role of AI in your creative work. Join the conversation by engaging with the concepts presented here, experimenting with AI tools, and sharing your experiences with others. Together, we can move from a place of fear to one of flourishing, embracing the future of creativity with open minds and hearts.

Welcome to "From Fear to Flourish: AI and the Future of Creativity." Let's embark on this transformative journey together.

Debunking the Myths

As AI continues to evolve and integrate into various aspects of our lives, it is accompanied by multiple misconceptions and fears. This chapter aims to debunk some of the most common myths about AI and creativity, helping you understand the true potential of AI as a creative tool.

Myth 1: AI Will Replace Creative Jobs

Why This Myth Exists:

The fear that AI will replace human jobs is not new. Every technological advancement, from the Industrial Revolution to the advent of computers, has sparked concerns about job displacement. In the realm of creativity, the fear is particularly acute because creative work is often seen as a deeply personal and human endeavor.

Why It's Wrong:

AI is designed to be a tool that enhances human capabilities, not replace them. Just as computers have not eliminated the need for writers, artists, and musicians, AI will not render creative professionals obsolete. Instead, it offers new ways to augment their work.

AI as a Tool for Enhancement:

AI can handle repetitive and mundane tasks, allowing creative professionals more time to focus on what they do best—creativity and innovation. For instance, AI can generate initial drafts, suggest improvements, and handle time-consuming edits, allowing writers to spend more time crafting compelling narratives.

Real-World Examples:

- **Writers:** AI tools like Grammarly and Hemingway can assist with editing, while language models like GPT-4 can generate content ideas or first drafts.
- **Artists:** AI-driven design tools can help with initial sketches and color palettes and even generate unique artwork that artists can refine.
- **Musicians:** AI can compose music or suggest melodies, providing a starting point for musicians to build upon.

Myth 2: AI Produces Soulless Work

Why This Myth Exists:

Creativity is often associated with emotional expression and personal experience. The idea that a machine could replicate or enhance this process seems counterintuitive to many.
Why It's Wrong: AI is not a replacement for human emotion and experience; it is a tool that can enhance and amplify these elements in creative work. The quality of AI-generated content heavily depends on the input it receives from human creators.

The Importance of Human Input:

AI models learn from vast datasets, but the human touch gives creative work its soul. Artists, writers, and musicians can use AI to explore new styles, experiment with different techniques, and push the boundaries of their creative expressions. The human creator remains at the center, guiding and refining the output to ensure it resonates emotionally and artistically.

Real-World Examples:

- **Visual Arts:** Artists use AI to generate new visual patterns and styles, which they then incorporate into their work, creating innovative and deeply personal pieces.
- **Writing:** Authors can use AI to brainstorm plot ideas, develop characters, and even simulate dialogue, all while infusing their unique voice and perspective into the final work.
- **Music:** AI can generate harmonies and rhythms that musicians may not have considered, offering new avenues for creativity and expression.

Myth 3: Everyone Will Become a Creator with AI

Why This Myth Exists: The democratization of technology often leads to fears of oversaturation and loss of quality. With AI tools becoming more accessible, there is a concern that everyone will be able to create, leading to an influx of mediocre content.

Why It's Wrong:

While AI does make creative tools more accessible, it does not automatically confer creative skills. Using AI effectively still requires knowledge, expertise, and an innovative mindset.

Skill and Mastery:

Just as owning a high-quality camera does not make someone a professional photographer, having access to AI tools does not make someone an accomplished artist, writer, or musician. The actual value of AI lies in its ability to enhance the skills of those who already possess a deep understanding of their craft.

Real-World Examples:

- **Photography:** AI can assist with photo editing and enhancement, but it is the photographer's eye for composition, lighting, and subject matter that creates a compelling image.
- **Writing:** AI can suggest ideas or generate text, but it is the writer's creativity, understanding of narrative structure, and ability to evoke emotion that makes a story engaging.
- **Music:** AI can compose basic melodies, but it is the musician's understanding of harmony, rhythm, and dynamics that turns these melodies into powerful music.

Embracing AI as a Creative Partner

To move from fear to flourishing, embracing AI as a partner in the creative process is essential. AI's strengths lie in its ability to process vast amounts of data, generate new ideas, and perform repetitive tasks quickly and accurately. By leveraging these strengths, creative professionals can push the boundaries of their work, explore new possibilities, and achieve greater levels of innovation and efficiency.

Practical Steps for Integration:

- **Experimentation:** Begin experimenting with AI tools in small projects to understand their capabilities and limitations.
- **Collaboration:** Use AI as a collaborative partner, integrating its suggestions and outputs into your creative process while maintaining your unique vision and style.
- **Continuous Learning:** Stay updated on the latest developments in AI technology and continually refine your skills to make the most of

these tools.

By debunking these myths and understanding the true potential of AI, we can shift our perspective from fear to opportunity. AI is not here to replace us but to enhance our creative abilities and open up new frontiers in art, writing, music, and beyond.

The Role of AI in Enhancing Creativity

As we move past the myths and misconceptions surrounding AI, it's time to delve into the tangible benefits and opportunities AI brings to the creative process. AI has the potential to transform how we create, offering tools and capabilities that enhance and expand our creative horizons. This chapter explores how AI can be integrated into creative workflows, providing real-world examples and practical advice for leveraging AI in art, writing, music, and design.

AI as a Creative Partner

Reimagining Collaboration:

In the traditional sense, creativity has often been a solitary endeavor or, at most, a collaborative effort among humans. AI introduces a new collaboration where human creativity and machine intelligence converge. This partnership allows for a dynamic interplay of ideas where AI can generate possibilities humans might not have considered.

Enhancing Idea Generation:

One of the primary ways AI enhances creativity is through idea generation. By analyzing vast amounts of data, AI can identify patterns, suggest new concepts, and predict trends. This capability is invaluable in the initial stages of the creative process, where brainstorming and exploration are crucial.

Case Study - Writing:

AI-powered tools like GPT-4 can help writers generate story ideas, develop characters, and outline plots. For example, a writer struggling with writer's block might input a few keywords or themes into an AI tool, which can then produce a range of story ideas or plot twists. The writer can then choose, refine, and build upon these suggestions, accelerating the creative process.

Case Studies: AI in Creative Industries

Visual Arts:

AI has made significant strides in the visual arts with tools that can generate unique artworks, assist with design, and even restore historical pieces. For instance, AI algorithms can analyze an artist's style and create new pieces similarly, offering a starting point for further refinement by the artist.

Example - DeepArt:

DeepArt is an AI tool that uses neural networks to turn photographs into artworks in the style of famous painters. Artists can upload their photos and choose a style, allowing the AI to generate a new piece that blends the original image with the artistic style selected. It not only saves time but also inspires new directions in their work.

Music:

In music, AI can compose, edit, and enhance musical pieces. AI tools are becoming indispensable in modern music production, from generating melodies and harmonies to mastering tracks.

Example - Amper Music:

Amper Music is an AI-driven platform that enables musicians to create custom music tracks. Users can specify the genre, mood, and instruments, and the AI generates a composition that meets these criteria. Musicians can then edit and refine the track, incorporating their unique style and expertise.

Design:

Designers benefit from AI's capabilities, with tools that can automate repetitive tasks, generate design variations, and optimize layouts.

Example - Adobe Sensei:

Adobe Sensei is an AI and machine learning framework integrated into Adobe's suite of creative tools. It helps designers by suggesting design elements, automating image tagging, and even predicting design trends. This allows designers to focus more on the creative aspects of their work while handling routine tasks more efficiently.

The Creative Process with AI

Integration into Workflow:

To fully harness the power of AI, it is essential to integrate it seamlessly into your creative workflow. It involves understanding the strengths and limitations of AI tools and knowing when and how to use them effectively.

Step-by-Step Guide:

- **Identify Tasks:** Determine which tasks in your creative process can benefit from AI assistance. These could be repetitive tasks, idea generation, or preliminary drafts.
- **Select Tools:** Choose the appropriate AI tools that align with your needs. Research and experiment with different options to find the best fit.
- **Experiment and Iterate:** Start using AI for small projects or parts of your process. Evaluate the results, adjust, and gradually expand its use as you become more comfortable.

- **Maintain Creative Control:** Remember that AI is a tool, not a replacement. Use it to augment your creativity, but ensure your unique voice and vision remain at the forefront.
- **Feedback Loop:** Continuously provide feedback to the AI tools you use. Many AI systems improve over time with more data and user interaction.

Real-World Examples

Advertising and Marketing:

In advertising, AI can analyze consumer data to generate personalized ad campaigns. AI can create content that resonates more deeply with target audiences by understanding audience preferences and behaviors.

Example - Persado:

Persado uses AI to create emotionally engaging marketing messages. Persado generates content that drives higher engagement and conversion rates by analyzing language patterns and consumer responses, allowing marketers to craft more effective campaigns.

Filmmaking:

AI is also making waves in filmmaking, from scriptwriting and editing to special effects and scene generation.

Example - ScriptBook:

ScriptBook is an AI tool that analyzes screenplays and predicts their success by evaluating plot structure, character development, and emotional impact. Filmmakers can use these insights to refine their scripts and improve their chances of success.

Challenges and Considerations

Balancing Creativity and Automation:

While AI offers many benefits, it is essential to balance automation and creativity. Over-reliance on AI can lead to homogenized content, so using AI as a supplement rather than a substitute for human creativity is crucial.

Ethical Considerations:

As with any technology, the use of AI in creative fields raises ethical questions. Authorship, originality, and the potential for bias in AI-generated content must be carefully considered. Creatives should remain vigilant about these concerns and strive for transparency and integrity in their work.

Looking Forward:

The future of AI in creativity is bright, with ongoing advancements promising even more sophisticated and powerful tools. By embracing AI as a creative partner, we can unlock new levels of innovation and expression, pushing the boundaries of what is possible in art, writing, music, and design.

In the next chapter, we will explore the specific AI tools available for different creative disciplines, providing a detailed guide on incorporating them into your work and maximizing their potential.

Tools of the Trade

As AI continues to revolutionize the creative industries, many tools have emerged to assist artists, writers, musicians, and designers in their work. This chapter will overview some of the most popular and effective AI tools available today, detailing their features and how they can be integrated into your creative process.

AI Tools for Writers

Grammarly:

Grammarly is an AI-powered writing assistant that helps with grammar, punctuation, and style. It offers real-time suggestions to improve clarity, conciseness, and tone. Beyond basic proofreading, Grammarly provides genre-specific writing style checks and helps ensure your writing is compelling and error-free.

Hemingway Editor:

The Hemingway Editor is a tool designed to make your writing clear and easy to read. It highlights complex sentences, passive voice, and adverbs, suggesting ways to make your writing more straightforward and impactful. The tool also provides readability scores, helping you tailor your content to your audience.

OpenAI GPT-4:

GPT-4 is a powerful language model capable of generating human-like text. Writers can brainstorm ideas, develop content, create dialogue, and even compose articles or stories. By providing prompts and refining outputs, writers can leverage GPT-4 to overcome writer's block and explore new creative directions.

Scrivener:

Scrivener is a writing software that integrates various AI functionalities to help writers organize their work. It offers plotting, character development, and manuscript formatting tools, making it an invaluable resource for novelists, screenwriters, and researchers.

AI in Visual Arts

DeepArt:

DeepArt uses neural networks to transform photos into artworks in the style of famous painters. Artists can upload their images and choose from various styles, allowing the AI to generate a unique piece that blends the original image with the artistic style selected.

DALL-E:

DALL-E, another creation by OpenAI, generates images from textual descriptions. Artists can input descriptions of scenes, objects, or styles, and DALL-E creates detailed images based on those inputs. This tool is excellent for visualizing concepts and generating inspiration for new projects.

Adobe Sensei:

Adobe Sensei is an AI and machine learning platform integrated into Adobe Creative Cloud applications like Photoshop, Illustrator, and Lightroom. It offers automated image tagging, content-aware fill, and design suggestions, streamlining the creative process and enhancing productivity.

Artbreeder:

Artbreeder allows artists to create and explore new visuals by blending images using generative adversarial networks (GANs). Users can combine different images to produce novel artworks, experiment with other styles, and explore endless creative possibilities.

AI in Music and Audio

Amper Music:

Amper Music is an AI-driven music composition tool that enables users to create custom music tracks. Users can generate compositions that fit their needs by specifying the genre, mood, and instrumentation. Musicians can then edit and refine these tracks, integrating their unique style and creativity.

AIVA (Artificial Intelligence Virtual Artist):

AIVA composes classical and symphonic music, making it an excellent tool for film scoring, video game soundtracks, and personal projects. Users can customize compositions based on their preferences, and AIVA provides sheet music and audio files for further use and performance.

LANDR:

LANDR is an AI-powered mastering tool that automates audio mastering. Musicians can upload their tracks, and LANDR applies mastering algorithms to enhance sound quality, ensuring the final product is polished and professional.

Magenta:

Magenta, developed by Google, is an open-source research project that explores the role of machine learning in the creative process. It provides tools and models for music generation, enabling musicians to experiment with AI-driven compositions and interactive music experiences.

AI in Video Production

Runway ML:

Runway ML offers AI tools for video editing, special effects, and real-time collaboration. It includes features like automated video masking, background removal, and style transfer, empowering video creators to produce high-quality content efficiently.

Lumen5:

Lumen5 is an AI-powered video creation platform that transforms text content into engaging videos. By analyzing the text and matching it with relevant visuals, music, and transitions, Lumen5 simplifies the video creation process for marketers, educators, and content creators.

Adobe Premiere Pro (with Adobe Sensei):

Adobe Premiere Pro integrates Adobe Sensei to offer AI-driven features like auto reframe, color matching, and scene editing. These tools help video editors streamline their workflow, making it easier to produce professional-quality videos.

DeepBrain AI:

DeepBrain AI offers tools for generating realistic digital avatars and deepfake technology. Video creators can use these tools to create lifelike virtual characters, automate dubbing and lip-syncing, and enhance visual storytelling.

Integrating AI Tools into Your Workflow

Step-by-Step Guide:

1. **Assess Your Needs:** Identify the areas of your creative process that could benefit from AI assistance. It might include idea generation, editing, design, composition, or video production.
2. **Research and Experiment:** Explore different AI tools and experiment with their features. Many tools offer free trials or basic versions that allow you to test their capabilities.
3. **Incorporate Gradually:** Start by integrating AI tools into small, manageable parts of your workflow. As you become more comfortable, expand their use to more complex tasks.
4. **Maintain Creative Control:** Use AI to enhance and streamline your work, but ensure your unique creative vision remains at the forefront. AI should be a tool that supports and amplifies your creativity, not replaces it.
5. **Stay Updated:** AI technology is constantly evolving. Keep up with the latest developments and updates to ensure you're using the most effective and innovative tools available.

Conclusion

AI tools offer incredible potential for enhancing creativity across various disciplines. Understanding and integrating these tools into your workflow can unlock new levels of innovation, efficiency, and artistic expression. The key is to embrace AI as a partner in your creative journey, leveraging its capabilities to complement and amplify your unique talents.

In the next chapter, we will explore the cultural and psychological barriers to adopting AI in creative work and provide strategies for overcoming these challenges, ensuring that you can fully embrace the transformative power of AI in your creative endeavors.

Overcoming Resistance

As we've explored, AI offers remarkable potential to enhance creativity and productivity across various fields. However, despite these benefits, resistance to adopting AI in creative processes remains significant. This chapter addresses the cultural and psychological barriers to AI adoption and provides strategies to overcome these challenges, ensuring you can fully embrace AI's transformative power.

Cultural and Psychological Barriers

Fear of the Unknown:

One of the primary reasons for resistance is the fear of the unknown. AI is a relatively new technology, and its rapid development can be intimidating. Many people need clarification on how it works, what it can do, and how it might impact their work and lives.

Loss of Control:

Creatives often need to gain control over their work when incorporating AI. The idea that a machine could make decisions traditionally made by humans can be unsettling. This fear is extreme in fields where personal touch and individuality are highly valued.

Threat to Job Security:

The misconception that AI will replace human jobs is a significant barrier. Many worry that AI will render their skills obsolete, leading to job loss and economic instability. This fear is compounded by high-profile stories of automation leading to layoffs in various industries.

Skepticism and Mistrust:

There is a natural skepticism towards new technologies, especially those that seem to creep into human creativity. Mistrust in AI's ability to produce quality, meaningful work makes many dismiss it as a gimmick rather than a valuable tool.

Ethical Concerns:

The ethical implications of AI, such as biases in AI algorithms and issues of authorship and originality, also contribute to resistance. Creatives are concerned about maintaining integrity and fairness while using AI tools.

Strategies for Overcoming Resistance

Education and Awareness:

Knowledge is the first step to overcoming fear and resistance. Understanding how AI works, capabilities, and limitations can demystify the technology and reduce anxiety. Educational resources, workshops, and hands-on experience with AI tools can help build confidence and competence.

Highlighting Success Stories:

Showcasing examples of successful AI integration in creative projects can inspire and motivate others. Case studies of artists, writers, musicians, and designers who have embraced and benefited from AI can serve as powerful testimonials.

Incremental Adoption:

Start small and gradually incorporate AI into your workflow. By beginning with less critical tasks and slowly expanding AI's role, you can build trust in the technology and adapt to its presence in your creative process.

Maintaining Creative Control:

It's essential to see AI as an enhancer rather than a replacer. Keep the final creative decisions in your hands, using AI to assist and amplify your work rather than dictate it. This approach ensures that your unique voice and vision remain central to your creations.

Collaboration and Community:

Engage with communities of creatives who are exploring AI. Sharing experiences, challenges, and successes can provide support and encouragement. Collaborative projects can also help mitigate the fear of isolation and foster a sense of shared growth and innovation.

Addressing Ethical Concerns:

Be proactive in understanding and addressing the ethical implications of AI. Ensure you use ethical AI tools, be aware of potential biases, and maintain transparency in your creative process. By doing so, you can uphold integrity and trustworthiness in your work.

Mindset Shifts

From Fear to Curiosity:

Shift your perspective from fear to curiosity. Instead of seeing AI as a threat, view it as an opportunity to explore new creative possibilities. Embrace a mindset of experimentation and discovery, allowing yourself to play and innovate with AI tools.

From Competition to Collaboration:

Recognize that AI is not a competitor but a collaborator. It is a tool designed to work with you, enhancing your abilities and extending your creative reach. This collaborative mindset can open up new avenues for creative expression and innovation.

From Resistance to Resilience:

Develop resilience in the face of technological change. Accept that the creative landscape is evolving and that adaptability is critical to thriving in this new environment. By being open to learning and growth, you can turn potential threats into opportunities for advancement.

From Scarcity to Abundance:

Adopt an abundance mindset, understanding that AI can create more opportunities than it takes away. AI can democratize creativity, making tools and resources available to a broader audience. This democratization can lead to a richer, more diverse creative landscape.

Practical Steps for Embracing AI

1. **Explore and Experiment:** Take the time to explore different AI tools and experiment with their features. Use free trials, attend workshops, and participate in online forums to learn and grow.
2. **Integrate Gradually:** Start by incorporating AI into specific parts of your creative process. Expand its use to more complex tasks and projects as you become more comfortable.
3. **Collaborate and Network:** Join communities of AI enthusiasts and creatives. Collaborate on projects, share insights, and learn from others' experiences.
4. **Stay Informed:** Keep up-to-date with the latest developments in AI technology. Subscribe to newsletters, follow industry leaders, and attend conferences to stay informed about new tools and trends.
5. **Reflect and Adapt:** Continuously reflect on your experience with AI. Assess what works, what doesn't, and how you can adapt to maximize the benefits of AI in your creative work.

Conclusion

Overcoming resistance to AI in creative work requires a combination of education, mindset shifts, and practical strategies. By addressing fears and misconceptions head-on, maintaining control over the creative process, and fostering a collaborative and curious mindset, you can unlock the full potential of AI as a powerful tool in your creative toolkit. The next chapter will explore future trends and predictions for AI in creativity, including emerging technologies and their potential impact on the creative industries. This forward-looking perspective will help you stay ahead of the curve and continue to innovate in your creative endeavors.

Future Trends and Predictions

The rapid advancement of AI technology has already begun to reshape the creative industries in profound ways. As we look to the future, we must understand the trends and predictions that will continue influencing and transforming the landscape of creativity. This chapter explores emerging technologies, potential impacts, and how to prepare to stay ahead in a constantly evolving environment.

The Evolution of AI in Creativity

Continued Advancements in AI Capabilities:

AI technology is evolving at an unprecedented pace. Future advancements will likely include more sophisticated algorithms that produce highly nuanced and context-aware creative outputs. AI can generate more realistic and emotionally resonant art, music, and literature as it learns to understand and mimic human emotions and experiences more accurately.

Increased Integration Across Disciplines:

We will see greater integration across creative disciplines as AI advances. Tools that combine visual art, music, writing, and design will enable creators to produce multidimensional works of art, seamlessly blending various media forms.

Example - AI-Powered Multimedia Projects:

- Imagine an AI system that can compose a soundtrack.
- Generate visual art.
- Write a narrative simultaneously, creating a cohesive multimedia experience.

This level of integration will open up new possibilities for cross-disciplinary collaboration and innovation.

Personalized Creativity

Customization and Personalization:

AI will enable unprecedented levels of customization and personalization in creative work. Creators can tailor their AI tools to match their unique styles, preferences, and creative goals. This personalization will enhance the creative process, making it more efficient and aligned with individual visions.

Example - Personalized AI Assistants:

Future AI tools might act as personal creative assistants, learning from your work habits, preferences, and feedback to provide increasingly relevant and tailored suggestions. These assistants could help you maintain consistency in your style while introducing fresh ideas and perspectives.

Audience-Specific Content:

AI will also allow creators to produce content tailored to different audience segments. By analyzing audience data and preferences, AI can help creators design works that resonate more deeply with specific groups, enhancing engagement and impact.

Example - Adaptive Storytelling:

In storytelling, AI could develop narratives that adapt to individual readers' or viewers' preferences and behaviors, creating highly personalized and immersive experiences.

Collaboration Between Humans and AI

Human-AI Co-Creation:

The future of creativity will likely involve even more seamless collaboration between humans and AI. Creators will work alongside AI as a tool and co-creator, leveraging AI's capabilities to explore new creative frontiers.

Example - AI in Music Production:

In music production, AI could collaborate with musicians in real-time, suggesting harmonies, rhythms, and lyrics as the musician composes. This dynamic interaction could lead to more innovative and unique compositions.

AI as a Creative Mentor:

AI could also serve as a mentor, providing guidance and feedback to emerging creators. AI could help individuals refine their skills and develop their creative voice by analyzing successful works and offering constructive critiques.

Example - AI Art Critique:

An AI system trained on thousands of pieces of art could provide insightful feedback to artists, highlighting strengths and suggesting areas for improvement based on a vast knowledge of artistic principles and techniques.

Ethical and Social Considerations

Addressing Bias and Fairness:

As AI becomes more integrated into creative processes, addressing bias and fairness issues will be crucial. Ensuring that AI-generated content is inclusive and representative of diverse perspectives will require ongoing attention and effort.

Example - Inclusive AI Training:

Developers must train AI systems on diverse datasets, incorporating various cultural, social, and artistic influences. This approach will help mitigate biases and ensure AI tools contribute to a more inclusive creative landscape.

Authorship and Intellectual Property:

The question of authorship and intellectual property will become increasingly complex as AI-generated content proliferates. Clear guidelines and regulations will be needed to determine the ownership and rights of AI-assisted creations.

ʌ.FEST..

Example - AI-Generated Art Ownership:

Who owns the final work if an AI generates art based on an artist's input? Establishing clear policies and legal frameworks will be essential to address these questions and protect the rights of creators.

Preparing for the Future

Continuous Learning and Adaptation:

Adopting a mindset of constant learning and adaptation is essential to stay ahead in the evolving creative landscape. Embrace new technologies, experiment with AI tools, and stay informed about the latest developments in the field.

Example - Lifelong Learning Programs:

Engage in lifelong learning programs, workshops, and courses focused on AI and creativity. These opportunities will help you stay current with technological advancements and enhance your skills.

Building a Collaborative Network:

Fostering a network of collaborators, including human and AI partners, will be crucial for future success. Collaborative projects and interdisciplinary partnerships can lead to innovative breakthroughs and expanded creative horizons.

Example - Interdisciplinary Creative Labs:

Participate in or establish creative labs that bring together artists, technologists, and researchers to explore the intersections of AI and creativity. These labs can serve as incubators for new ideas and collaborative projects.

Embracing Ethical Practices:

As you integrate AI into your creative work, prioritize ethical considerations. Ensure transparency in using AI, address potential biases, and strive for inclusivity and fairness in your creations.

Example - Ethical AI Guidelines:

Develop and adhere to ethical guidelines for using AI in your creative practice. These guidelines should outline fairness, transparency, and inclusivity principles, helping you navigate the moral complexities of AI-assisted creativity.

Conclusion

The future of creativity is bright, with AI offering unprecedented opportunities for innovation and expression. By staying informed about emerging trends and technologies, embracing ethical practices, and fostering collaborative networks, you can navigate the evolving landscape and harness the full potential of AI in your creative work.

In the next chapter, we will delve into personal stories and testimonials from creatives who have successfully integrated AI into their work. These insights will provide practical examples and inspiration for your journey from fear to flourishing in the age of AI-enhanced creativity.

Personal Stories and Testimonials

The transformative potential of AI in creativity is best illustrated through the experiences of individuals who have embraced this technology in their work. This chapter presents personal stories and testimonials from artists, writers, musicians, and designers who have integrated AI into their creative processes. Their journeys provide valuable insights and inspiration for anyone looking to move from fear to flourishing in the age of AI-enhanced creativity.

Stories from Artists

Elena Thompson: The AI Collaborator

Elena Thompson, a digital artist, was initially skeptical about using AI in her work. She feared it would strip her art of its uniqueness and personal touch. However, after experimenting with AI tools like DeepArt and DALL-E, Elena discovered new avenues for creative exploration.

Testimonial: "*I started using DeepArt to transform some of my sketches into styles I had never considered before. The AI didn't replace my creativity; it expanded it. It gave me new perspectives and ideas that I could incorporate into my work. Now, I see AI as a collaborator, not a competitor. It has enriched my artistic process and pushed me to explore beyond my comfort zone.*"

Raj Patel: The Multimedia Innovator

A multimedia artist, Raj Patel uses AI to create immersive experiences that blend visual art, music, and storytelling. By leveraging AI tools like Runway ML and OpenAI's GPT-4, Raj creates interactive installations that engage audiences in novel ways.

Testimonial: "*AI has allowed me to break down the barriers between different forms of art. With tools like Runway ML, I can generate visuals that respond to music created by AI, while GPT-4 helps me craft narratives that tie everything together. The synergy between AI and human creativity in my installations has been transformative. It's a dance between man and machine, each enhancing the other's performance."*

Stories from Writers

Sophia Martinez: Overcoming Writer's Block

Sophia Martinez, a novelist, struggled with writer's block for years. Frustrated with her inability to progress, she turned to AI tools like GPT-4 for inspiration. By inputting basic plot outlines and character descriptions, Sophia received suggestions and ideas that helped her progress with her writing.

Testimonial: "I was amazed at how GPT-4 could generate plot twists and dialogue that felt natural and intriguing. It wasn't perfect, but it provided the spark I needed to get past my block. AI didn't write my book for me, but it acted as a catalyst for my creativity. Now, I use it regularly to brainstorm and refine my ideas."

David Lee: Crafting Personalized Stories

David Lee, a content creator, uses AI to craft personalized stories for his audience. By analyzing reader preferences and feedback, David employs AI to tailor his stories to individual tastes, creating a more engaging and customized reading experience.

Testimonial: "Using AI, I can analyze what my readers enjoy and incorporate those elements into my stories. It's like having a direct line to their preferences. AI helps me understand my audience better and create content that resonates with them deeper. The feedback has been overwhelmingly positive, and I feel more connected to my readers than ever before."

Stories from Musicians

Alex Chen: Composing with AI

Alex Chen, a composer and music producer, integrates AI into his music creation process. Using tools like Amper Music and AIVA, Alex experiments with different genres and styles, pushing the boundaries of his musical creativity.

Testimonial: "AI has opened up a world of possibilities for me. With Amper Music, I can compose tracks in genres I'm less familiar with, and AIVA helps me generate orchestral compositions that would take me weeks to write on my own. AI doesn't replace my creativity; it enhances it. It's like having an endless source of inspiration and technical support at my fingertips."

Lisa Nguyen: Real-Time Music Collaboration

Lisa Nguyen, a live performer, uses AI to enhance her performances. Lisa creates dynamic and interactive live shows by incorporating AI-driven tools that generate harmonies and rhythms in real time.

Testimonial: "Performing with AI is exhilarating. It's like having an extra band member who can anticipate and adapt to what I'm doing. The real-time collaboration between me and the AI adds a layer of spontaneity and excitement to my performances. It's a unique experience for me and my audience, keeping my shows fresh and innovative."

Stories from Designers

Emma Johnson: Design Efficiency and Innovation

A graphic designer, Emma Johnson leverages AI tools like Adobe Sensei to streamline her workflow and enhance her designs. By automating repetitive tasks and generating design suggestions, Emma can focus more on the creative aspects of her projects.

Testimonial: "Adobe Sensei has revolutionized the way I work. It takes care of the mundane tasks, like resizing images and color matching, allowing me to spend more time on the creative elements. The design suggestions are also incredibly helpful, sparking new ideas and helping me push my designs further. AI has made me more efficient and more innovative in my work."

Carlos Alvarez: AI-Driven User Experience Design

Carlos Alvarez, a UX/UI designer, uses AI to create user-centered, functional, and aesthetically pleasing designs. AI helps Carlos design interfaces that enhance the user experience by analyzing user behavior and preferences.

Testimonial: *"AI tools allow me to gain deeper insights into user behavior, which I can translate into better design decisions. Whether it's through heatmaps or predictive analytics, AI provides valuable data that informs my design process. The result is a more intuitive and enjoyable user experience. AI is an indispensable part of my toolkit, helping me create designs that truly resonate with users."*

Lessons Learned and Advice

Embrace Experimentation:

Each of these creatives has learned the value of experimentation. By being open to trying new tools and approaches, they discovered how AI could enhance their work.

Balance and Integration:

The key to successful AI integration is balance. Maintaining control over the creative process while leveraging AI's strengths leads to the best outcomes.

Continuous Learning:

Staying informed about the latest AI developments and continuously learning how to use new tools effectively is crucial for maximizing their potential.

Community and Collaboration:

Engaging with a community of like-minded creatives who are also exploring AI can provide support, inspiration, and valuable insights.

Conclusion

The personal stories and testimonials shared in this chapter highlight the transformative impact of AI on creativity. These experiences demonstrate that AI can be a powerful ally, enhancing and expanding the creative capabilities of artists, writers, musicians, and designers. By embracing AI, you, too, can unlock new levels of innovation and expression in your work.

In the next chapter, we will explore practical applications of AI in various creative fields, providing step-by-step guides and examples to help you integrate AI into your projects effectively.

**Practical Applications**

After examining the transformative potential of AI in creativity through personal stories and testimonials, this chapter delves into the practical applications of AI across various creative fields. We will provide step-by-step guides and examples to help you integrate AI effectively into your projects, enhancing your creativity and productivity.

AI in Writing

Generating Content Ideas

Step-by-Step Guide:

1. **Identify the Topic:** Start with a broad topic or theme you want to explore.
2. **Use AI for Brainstorming:** Tools like GPT-4 can help generate a list of potential subtopics, plot points, or character ideas.
3. **Refine Ideas:** Review the AI-generated suggestions and select the ones that resonate with you. Refine these ideas to fit your unique voice and style.
4. **Create an Outline:** Use the selected ideas to create an outline for your project, providing a clear roadmap for your writing process.

Example:

Suppose you're writing a science fiction novel. Input your central theme (e.g., "colonizing Mars") into GPT-4 and receive suggestions like "challenges of terraforming," "interpersonal conflicts among settlers," and "unexpected discoveries." Use these ideas to structure your story and develop plotlines.

Enhancing Editing and Proofreading

Step-by-Step Guide:

1. **Draft Your Work:** Write your initial draft without worrying about minor errors.
2. **Use AI Tools:** Employ tools like Grammarly and Hemingway Editor to analyze your text for grammar, punctuation, and style improvements.
3. **Review Suggestions:** Carefully review the AI-generated suggestions and decide which ones to implement based on your writing goals
4. **Refine and Polish:** Make the necessary adjustments and polish your draft, ensuring clarity and readability.

Example:

After drafting an article, run it through Grammarly to catch grammatical errors and Hemingway Editor to improve readability. These tools help you produce a polished final piece with minimal effort.

AI in Visual Arts

Creating Digital Art

Step-by-Step Guide:

1. **Choose Your Tool:** Select an AI tool like DeepArt or DALL-E.
2. **Input Source Material:** Upload a photo or sketch you want to transform.
3. **Select Style:** Choose an artistic style or provide a textual description for the transformation.
4. **Generate Artwork:** Let the AI create the artwork based on your inputs.
5. **Refine the Output:** Adjust the AI-generated piece to align it with your vision.

Example:

Upload a landscape photo to DeepArt and select the style of Vincent van Gogh. The AI transforms your photo into a painting reminiscent of Van Gogh's style. You can then refine the artwork using your digital art software.

Enhancing Graphic Design

Step-by-Step Guide:

1. **Start with a Concept:** Develop a rough concept or idea for your design project.
2. **Use AI Tools for Inspiration:** Tools like Adobe Sensei can suggest design elements, color palettes, and layouts.
3. **Generate Variations:** Experiment with different design variations generated by the AI.
4. **Select and Refine:** Choose and refine the most compelling designs to suit your project's needs.

Example:

Use Adobe Sensei to generate multiple poster layouts for a marketing campaign. Please select and customize the most visually appealing designs to fit your brand's aesthetic and message.

AI in Music and Audio

Composing Music

Step-by-Step Guide:

1. **Define Your Genre and Mood:** Determine the genre and mood you want for your composition.
2. **Use AI Tools:** Tools like Amper Music or AIVA can generate music based on your specifications.
3. **Review and Edit:** Listen to the AI-generated music and make adjustments to ensure it aligns with your creative vision.
4. **Add Personal Touches:** Incorporate your unique style by adding or modifying instrumental parts, harmonies, and rhythms.

Example:

Using Amper Music, create a background score for a short film by selecting the genre (e.g., orchestral) and mood (e.g., suspenseful). Edit the generated score to match your film's pacing and emotional tone.

Enhancing Live Performances

Step-by-Step Guide:

1. **Set Up Your Equipment:** Ensure you have the equipment for live performance, including AI tools like those in Runway ML.
2. **Integrate AI Tools:** Use AI tools to generate live visual effects or real-time music harmonies.
3. **Rehearse with AI:** Practice your performance with the AI to ensure smooth integration and timing.
4. **Perform and Adjust:** During the performance, make real-time adjustments to the AI-generated elements to enhance the overall experience.

Example:

In a live DJ set, use Runway ML to create real-time visual effects that sync with the music. Adjust the fly's visuals to match the crowd's energy and mood.

AI in Video Production

Editing and Enhancing Videos

Step-by-Step Guide:

1. **Import Your Footage:** Import your raw footage into video editing software that supports AI, like Adobe Premiere Pro with Adobe Sensei.
2. **Use AI Features:** Utilize AI features for tasks like auto-reframing, color correction, and scene detection.
3. **Please review and Adjust:** Check the AI-generated edits and make any necessary adjustments to ensure they meet your creative standards.
4. **Finalize and Export:** Once satisfied with the edits, finalize your video and export it in the desired format.

Example:

Edit a travel vlog using Adobe Sensei's auto-reframe to optimize shots for different social media platforms. Apply AI-driven color correction to enhance the visual appeal of your footage.

Creating Animated Videos

Step-by-Step Guide:

1. **Develop a Script:** Write a script or storyboard for your animated video.
2. **Use AI Animation Tools:** Tools like DeepBrain AI can help generate realistic animations and avatars based on your script.
3. **Integrate Voice and Sound:** Add voiceovers and sound effects, using AI tools for dubbing and lip-syncing if needed.
4. **Review and Refine:** Watch the AI-generated animation and refine any elements to ensure they align with your vision.
5. **Publish and Share:** Finalize and share your animated video across your platforms.

Example:

Create an educational video using DeepBrain AI to animate a virtual teacher explaining complex concepts. Integrate AI-generated voiceovers for clear and engaging narration.

AI in Design

User Experience (UX) Design

Step-by-Step Guide:

1. **Conduct User Research:** Gather data on user preferences and behaviors.
2. **Use AI Analytics:** Employ AI tools to analyze user data and generate insights.
3. **Design Prototypes:** Create UX prototypes using AI-powered design tools that suggest optimal layouts and elements.
4. **Test and Iterate:** Use AI to conduct A/B testing and gather feedback. Iterate your design based on user responses and AI recommendations.
5. **Implement and Launch:** Finalize and implement your design in your product, ensuring a seamless user experience.

Example:

Design a mobile app interface by analyzing user behavior data with an AI tool. Use the insights to create prototypes that optimize user engagement and satisfaction.

Graphic Design Automation

Step-by-Step Guide:

1. **Define Project Goals:** Outline the objectives and requirements for your graphic design project.
2. **Input Parameters into AI Tools:** Use tools like Canvas Magic Resize or Adobe Spark to generate design variations based on your specifications.
3. **Review AI Outputs:** Evaluate the AI-generated designs and select the ones that best meet your project goals.
4. **Customize and Finalize:** The selected designs to ensure they align with your brand and vision.
5. **Produce and Distribute:** Produce and distribute the final designs across your desired channels.

Example:

Create a series of social media posts for a marketing campaign using Adobe Spark. Input your brand's colors, fonts, and messaging to generate multiple post variations. Customize and finalize the best designs for your campaign.

Conclusion

AI offers a wealth of tools and possibilities to enhance creativity across various fields. By understanding and integrating these tools into your workflow, you can unlock new levels of innovation and efficiency. The practical applications outlined in this chapter provide a starting point for incorporating AI into your creative projects, helping you achieve more with less effort.

The next chapter will explore ways to expand your creative horizons by collaborating with others and combining different fields and AI technologies. This collaborative approach will help you push the boundaries of what's possible and continue to innovate in your creative endeavors.

Expanding Your Creative Horizons

As we continue to explore the integration of AI into creative processes, it becomes clear that the true potential of this technology lies not just in individual applications but in the collaborative and interdisciplinary opportunities it creates. This chapter will explore strategies for expanding your creative horizons by embracing collaboration, exploring cross-disciplinary creativity, and building supportive networks.

Collaborative Projects

The Power of Collaboration:

Collaboration can significantly enhance creativity by bringing together diverse perspectives, skills, and ideas. AI can facilitate and augment collaboration by providing tools that streamline communication, project management, and the creative process.

Collaborating with AI:

Using AI tools as collaborative partners can open new creative avenues. For example, writers can collaborate with AI to develop story ideas, while musicians can use AI to experiment with new sounds and compositions.

Example - Virtual Jam Sessions:

Musicians worldwide can create virtual jam sessions using AI-driven platforms. Tools like Amper Music can generate backing tracks, allowing musicians to focus on improvisation and collaboration in real time, regardless of physical distance.

Human-to-Human Collaboration with AI:

AI can also facilitate collaboration between human creators by handling repetitive tasks and generating preliminary drafts or prototypes, allowing collaborators to focus on refining and enhancing the final product.

Example - Co-Authoring Books:

Authors can use AI tools to generate initial drafts of chapters or sections, which they can then collaboratively edit and refine. This approach can speed up the writing process and introduce fresh perspectives that enhance the final work.

Cross-Disciplinary Creativity

Breaking Down Silos:

One of the most exciting aspects of AI in creativity is its ability to break down traditional silos between disciplines. By integrating tools and techniques from different fields, creators can develop innovative works that transcend conventional boundaries.

Example - Art and Technology:

An artist might collaborate with a technologist to create interactive installations that respond to viewer movements using AI-driven sensors and algorithms. This fusion of art and technology creates immersive experiences that engage audiences in new ways.

Exploring New Mediums:

AI enables creators to experiment with new mediums and formats, expanding their creative repertoire. For instance, a writer might use AI-generated illustrations or animations to explore visual storytelling.

Example - Interactive Storytelling:

Using AI tools, a writer can develop interactive stories that allow readers to make choices that influence the narrative. AI algorithms can generate plot paths based on reader decisions, creating a dynamic and personalized reading experience.

Case Study - AI-Generated Music Videos:

A musician might collaborate with a visual artist to produce AI-generated music videos. By inputting the music track into an AI tool like Runway ML, the team can create visuals synchronizing with the music, resulting in a cohesive and visually stunning piece.

Building a Supportive Network

The Importance of Community:

Building a supportive network of like-minded creators is crucial for staying inspired and motivated. Engaging with a community provides opportunities for feedback, collaboration, and learning.

Online Communities and Forums:

Join online communities and forums where creatives discuss AI and share their experiences. Platforms like Reddit, Discord, and specialized forums offer spaces for creators to connect, share resources, and seek advice.

Example - AI Art Communities:

Participate in AI art communities where artists share their work, discuss techniques, and collaborate on projects. These communities can provide valuable insights and inspiration for your creative endeavors.

Workshops and Conferences:

Attend workshops and conferences focused on AI and creativity. These events offer opportunities to learn from experts, network with peers, and stay updated on the latest trends and technologies.

Example - AI Creativity Conference:

Participate in conferences like the AI Creativity Conference, where artists, technologists, and researchers come together to discuss the impact of AI on creative industries. These events often feature keynote speakers, panel discussions, and hands-on workshops.

Fostering Innovation Through Experimentation

Embrace a Growth Mindset:

Cultivating a growth mindset is essential for innovation. Embrace experimentation and be open to failure as a learning process. AI tools provide a sandbox for creative exploration, allowing you to test ideas without significant investment.

Iterative Process:

Adopt an iterative process in your creative work. Use AI to generate initial concepts, then refine and enhance these ideas through multiple iterations. This approach encourages continuous improvement and innovation.

Example - Design Thinking with AI:

Apply design thinking principles to your creative process, using AI tools to prototype and test ideas quickly. Gather feedback from collaborators and iterate on your designs to develop innovative solutions.

Creative Sprints:

Organize creative sprints where you and your collaborators focus intensively on generating and developing ideas using AI tools. These short, focused bursts of creativity can lead to breakthroughs and innovative concepts.

Example - Hackathons:

Participate in or organize hackathons that bring together creators from various disciplines to solve creative challenges using AI. These events foster collaboration, rapid prototyping, and the development of innovative solutions.

Expanding Your Skill Set

Learning New Tools:

Stay updated with the latest AI tools and technologies relevant to your field. Continuously expand your skill set to incorporate new techniques and approaches into your creative process.

Online Courses and Tutorials:

Take advantage of online courses and tutorials to learn how to use AI tools effectively. Platforms like Coursera, Udemy, and YouTube offer a wealth of resources for learning about AI and its applications in creativity.

Example - AI Art and Design Courses:

Enroll in courses that teach AI art and design techniques, such as using neural networks for image generation or applying machine learning algorithms to design projects. These courses help you develop new skills and stay competitive.

Collaborative Learning:

Engage in collaborative learning experiences where you can learn from and with others. Join study groups, participate in online challenges, and collaborate on projects that push the boundaries of your creativity.

Example - AI Creative Challenges:

Participate in AI creative challenges and competitions where creators use AI tools to develop innovative works. These challenges provide opportunities to learn, experiment, and showcase your skills.

Conclusion

Expanding your creative horizons with AI involves embracing collaboration, exploring cross-disciplinary opportunities, and building a supportive network. By adopting a growth mindset and continuously growing your skill set, you can leverage AI to push the boundaries of what's possible and continue to innovate in your creative endeavors.

In the final chapter, we will reflect on the journey from fear to flourishing, offering a recap of key insights and encouraging you to embrace the future of creativity with confidence and excitement.

Conclusion

As we conclude this journey through the transformative potential of AI in the creative industries, we must reflect on the insights we've gained and look forward to the exciting future ahead. This chapter recaps the critical themes explored in this book and encourages you to embrace AI as a powerful ally in your creative endeavors.

Reflecting on the Journey

From Fear to Understanding:

We addressed common fears and misconceptions about AI. These fears, while understandable, often stem from a lack of understanding of what AI truly represents. By debunking myths and providing a clearer picture of AI's capabilities, we've laid the groundwork for a more informed and optimistic perspective.

Embracing AI as a Tool:

AI is not here to replace human creativity but to enhance it. Throughout this book, we've seen how AI can be a valuable tool in various creative fields, from writing and visual arts to music and design. By automating repetitive tasks, generating new ideas, and offering fresh perspectives, AI empowers creators to focus on what they do best: being creative.

Personal Stories of Transformation:

The personal stories and testimonials shared in this book highlight the real-world impact of AI on individual creators. These narratives demonstrate that AI can be a catalyst for overcoming creative blocks, expanding creative boundaries, and achieving new levels of innovation. Key Insights

Collaboration Over Competition:

AI thrives as a collaborative partner. Rather than viewing AI as a competitor, embracing it as a collaborator can open new creative possibilities. The synergy between human intuition and machine intelligence can lead to groundbreaking work that neither could achieve alone.

Cross-Disciplinary Creativity:

AI facilitates cross-disciplinary creativity by breaking down silos and encouraging the fusion of different artistic and technological domains. This interdisciplinary approach can lead to innovative projects pushing traditional creative practices' boundaries.

Continuous Learning and Adaptation:

The world of AI is constantly evolving, and staying ahead requires a commitment to constant learning and adaptation. By keeping up with the latest developments and being open to experimenting with new tools and techniques, creators can harness the full potential of AI.

Ethical Considerations:

As we integrate AI into our creative processes, it is crucial to consider the moral implications. Ensuring fairness, transparency, and inclusivity in AI-generated content is essential for maintaining integrity and trust in our work.

Encouragement for the Future

Embrace the Unknown:

The future of AI in creativity is filled with unknowns, but this uncertainty should be seen as an opportunity rather than a threat. Embrace the unknown with curiosity and a willingness to explore new horizons. The creative landscape is expanding, and those willing to adapt and innovate will lead the way.

Lead with Your Unique Vision:

AI is a powerful tool, but it is your unique vision, creativity, and personal touch that will set your work apart. Use AI to amplify your strengths and bring your ideas to life in ways that were previously unimaginable. Build a Supportive Network: Surround yourself with a community of like-minded creators who are also exploring the possibilities of AI.

Collaborate, share insights, and support each other in your creative journeys. Together, you can navigate the evolving landscape and achieve greater heights.

Stay Ethical and Inclusive:

As you leverage AI in your work, remain committed to ethical practices. Ensure that your use of AI is transparent, fair, and inclusive. By doing so, you contribute to a creative, innovative, but also just and equitable future.

Final Thoughts

The journey from fear to flourishing with AI is a transformative one. You can unlock new levels of creativity and innovation by understanding AI's true potential, embracing it as a creative partner, and staying committed to continuous learning and ethical practices. The future of creativity is bright, and AI is a powerful ally on this journey.

Thank you for embarking on this exploration with us. We hope this book has inspired you to embrace AI with confidence and excitement, and we look forward to seeing the incredible work you will create as you continue to push the boundaries of what's possible.

Welcome to the future of creativity. Let's flourish together.

**Appendices**

Resources and Further Reading

To deepen your understanding of AI and its impact on creativity, here is a curated list of books, articles, and online resources that offer valuable insights and practical knowledge.

Books:

1. **"Artificial Intelligence: A Guide for Thinking Humans" by Melanie Mitchell**
   - A comprehensive introduction to AI, its capabilities, and its societal implications.
2. **"The Creativity Code: How AI is Learning to Write, Paint, and Think" by Marcus du Sautoy**
   - An exploration of how AI is used in various creative fields and its potential to transform creativity.
3. **"You Look Like a Thing and I Love You: How AI Works and Why It's Making the World a Weirder Place" by Janelle Shane**
   - A humorous and insightful look at how AI works and its often unexpected results.
4. **"Deep Learning" by Ian Goodfellow, Yoshua Bengio, and Aaron Courville**
   - A foundational text on profound learning principles, a key technology behind many AI applications in creativity.
5. **"AI Superpowers: China, Silicon Valley, and the New World Order" by Kai-Fu Lee**
   - An analysis of the global AI race and its implications for the future of work and creativity.

Articles:

1. **"The Role of Artificial Intelligence in Creativity" - MIT Technology Review**
   - An article discussing the impact of AI on creative industries and future possibilities.

2. **"How AI is Revolutionizing Art and Creativity" - Forbes**
   - Insights into how artists and creators use AI tools to push the boundaries of their work.
3. **"AI and Creativity: Why Algorithms Won't Replace Artists" - The Guardian**
   - A perspective on why human creativity remains essential even as AI becomes more advanced.
4. **"The Ethics of AI in Creative Work" - Harvard Business Review**
   - Discuss the ethical considerations and challenges of using AI in creative fields.
5. **"AI in Music: From Composition to Production" - Rolling Stone**
   - An exploration of how AI is transforming the music industry.

Online Resources:

1. **Coursera: AI for Everyone by Andrew Ng**
   - An accessible online course that provides a broad overview of AI, suitable for beginners.
2. **OpenAI Blog**
   - Updates, research, and insights from one of the leading organizations in AI development.
3. **DeepArt Website**
   - A platform for creating AI-generated artworks based on user-uploaded photos and selected styles.
4. **Magenta Studio**
   - Tools and resources from Google's Magenta project, focusing on AI-generated music and art.
5. **Runway ML**
   - A suite of AI tools for artists, designers, and creators, including tutorials and community projects.

Glossary of Terms

- **AI (Artificial Intelligence):** The simulation of human intelligence processes by machines, especially computer systems.
- **Algorithm:** A process or rules a computer follows in problem-solving operations.

- **Deep Learning:** A subset of machine learning involving neural networks with many layers, allowing computers to learn from large amounts of data.
- **Generative Adversarial Networks (GANs):** A class of AI algorithms used to generate images, music, and other data by training two neural networks.
- **Machine Learning:** A subset of AI that involves training algorithms to learn from and make predictions or decisions based on data.
- **Natural Language Processing (NLP):** A field of AI that focuses on the interaction between computers and human language, enabling computers to understand, interpret, and generate human language.
- **Neural Network:** A series of algorithms that mimic the operations of a human brain to recognize patterns and solve common problems in AI.
- **Predictive Analytics:** Using statistical algorithms and machine learning techniques to identify the likelihood of future outcomes based on historical data.
- **Style Transfer:** An AI technique that applies one image's visual style to another's content, often used in digital art.
- **Training Data:** The dataset trains an AI model, allowing it to learn patterns and make decisions.